MOTOCROSS RACING

John Perritano

Rourke
Educational Media

rourkeeducationalmedia.com

Before Reading:

Building Academic Vocabulary and Background Knowledge

Before reading a book, it is important to tap into what your child or students already know about the topic. This will help them develop their vocabulary, increase their reading comprehension, and make connections across the curriculum.

1. *Look at the cover of the book. What will this book be about?*
2. *What do you already know about the topic?*
3. *Let's study the Table of Contents. What will you learn about in the book's chapters?*
4. *What would you like to learn about this topic? Do you think you might learn about it from this book? Why or why not?*
5. *Use a reading journal to write about your knowledge of this topic. Record what you already know about the topic and what you hope to learn about the topic.*
6. *Read the book.*
7. *In your reading journal, record what you learned about the topic and your response to the book.*
8. *After reading the book complete the activities below.*

Content Area Vocabulary
Read the list. What do these words mean?

checkered flag
cylinder
diffused
exhibition
exploits
fiberglass
maneuver
spark plug
suspension system
terrain
throttle
traction
variations

After Reading:

Comprehension and Extension Activity

After reading the book, work on the following questions with your child or students in order to check their level of reading comprehension and content mastery.

1. *Early motocross in Europe only obtained speeds of 24 miles per hour. Why do you think they would not go faster? (Infer)*
2. *Explain how FMX got started. (Summarize)*
3. *Do you have what it takes to be a motocross racer? Explain. (Text to self connection)*
4. *How does the course affect how a racer trains? (Summarize)*
5. *Why would riders choose a two-stroke engine versus a four-stroke engine? (Asking questions)*

Extension Activity

There are similarities and differences between the different types of motocross. Using the text, compare and contrast two types of motocross. Create a Venn diagram to organize your information. Which type of motocross do you like best? Why?

TABLE OF CONTENTS

ALL REVVED UP

Ken Roczen knows the drill well. He feels excitement, energy, and just a little bit of nerves. The expert motocross rider has competed at Angel Stadium in Anaheim, California, before. The track has been good to him. He's won here twice in four races. Today, he goes for his third victory. He looks across the crowded field of riders. Will this again be his day? Ken hopes so.

The race begins with the scream of motors and the shifting of gears. Sitting on his Suzuki, Ken grips the **throttle** and lets it unwind. The 20-year-old German quickly falls behind. He's in second place. The first curves belong to Andrew Short. No worries. Ken lets loose. Not since the days of Travis Pastrana and Rickey Carmichael has a young rider exploded on the motocross circuit with such skill. Still, Ken has to win the races. Today is no different. He puts his head down and goes for speed!

GETTING STARTED

Off-road motocross riding can include jumps over obstacles.

Go as fast as you can go, during practice and during every race–that's the goal of the motocross rider. You've trained hard. Your bike is tuned up. The engine hums. That's a good start. What about your mind? Is that tuned up, too? A fast bike is important. To win, however, you have to be mentally tough and confident. Are you?

Motocross demands a lot. Racers have to be physically fit and cannot doubt their skills or abilities. They need to focus on what's in front of them, what's alongside, and what's behind them. At the end of the race, though, all racers want to be alone at the finish line, a **checkered flag** waving in their face.

Motocross is not just a hobby. Whether it's SuperMoto, Supercross, or other **variations**, motocross is a way of life. It's one of the most exciting forms of motor sports.

Motocross riders never let a little mud puddle—or a big one—get in their way.

This 1924 magazine ad features a motorcycle used in the Scott Scramble.

HISTORY

Motocross began in the 1920s on the hilly fields of Europe. The first motocross race was held in England in 1924. On a March day just outside of London, 80 riders gathered for the Southern Scott Scramble. The event did not resemble anything like today's races. Riders plodded 50 miles (80 kilometers) on a rugged 2.5 mile (4 kilometer) course. The course was so tough that it humbled the best of them. A local rider, Arthur Sparks, won the race. He needed two hours to complete the circuit. The average speed that day was 24 miles (38.6 kilometers) per hour.

Despite the turtle-like pace of the sport, motocross—it was called the scramble back then—was born. It spread quickly to Belgium and France. At the same time, a few Americans were racing in the United States, not on rocky hills but on dirt tracks.

No Brakes

The name motocross comes from combining *motorcycle* and *cross country*. Early racing bikes did not have brakes. Bikers raced with their throttles wide open.

Edison Dye's Flying Circus

After watching Torsten Hallman race in Europe, and looking at the reactions of fans, Edison Dye, who ran a trucking business, had an idea. He brought Torsten and other European racers to America. They raced around the country in Edison Dye's Flying Circus. Americans loved the European brand of motocross.

The group held events called Gypsy Tours on weekends. Riders rode to a single location to have a picnic and to race. Though a small group of American riders competed in AMA races in the 1960s, the sport had yet to find a wider audience.

Edison Dye (1918–2007)

Courtesy of Tom White

That all changed in 1966 when Torsten Hallman, a Swedish rider, came to the US. Torsten was a European champion. He rode a type of motorcycle called Husqvarna at a number of **exhibition** events in the US and Canada. American riders were thrilled. So were the fans. The press loved Torsten and his **exploits** made headlines. Motocross (MX) in the United States was here to stay.

Torsten Hallman (1939–)

Smaller 250cc motorcycles use a two-stroke engine.

Today, the AMA Motocross championship is the top American motocross series. The series features 12 races on tracks that are nothing like the old European courses. Modern riders have to navigate human-made obstacles including a series of jumps. Each race features 20 to 40 riders. They line up twice a day to race two motos, or races.

When all the races are over, the finishing positions of each rider are added up. The racer with the lowest score wins. Two main classes are in the AMA Motocross and Supercross Championship Series: the 250cc two-stroke and the 450cc four-stroke. Each class is named for the size and type of the bike's engine.

The mighty 450cc bikes are the standard for the highest levels of motocross.

SPORTS SKILLS

To drive a motorcycle, riders use one hand for the throttle to make the bike go. The other hand controls one of the brakes. But motocross is not a Sunday ride down Main Street. Motocross racers not only have to know how to ride, they have to know how to jump. They learn to take advantage of any situation on the track. They must also be

Most riders use their right hand to throttle and their left hand for the brake.

in great shape. Riders have to be able to race for 30 minutes while maneuvering vehicles that weigh more than 200 pounds (90.7 kilograms). The track is nearly a mile (1.6 kilometers) long and made of loose dirt, sand, or clay—not the easiest surfaces to ride on.

Racers are generally well-built and strong. They need to know how to breathe correctly while bouncing through the bumps so their body can have enough oxygen. Many drivers also lift weights to become stronger, focusing on their arms, especially their forearms. That's because drivers have to use their forearms to throttle, brake, and **maneuver** their bikes on courses that often resemble the surface of the Moon.

Riders need strength from their bodies as well as their bikes to rumble over rocks.

While fans cheer from stadium seats, Supercross riders race in a pack on a bumpy, twisting track.

Although motocross was invented in Europe, Supercross is all-American. The stadium-racing competition was born in 1972 at the Los Angeles Coliseum in California. Some historians say there were other stadium events in Europe during the late 1940s. Still, Supercross is an American original, a hit with cycle-crazy fans that pack stadiums to watch races.

Supercross is the highest level of motocross. Unlike motocross courses, Supercross tracks are enclosed in stadiums. They're built with tight U-turns and a series of whoop-de-doos, which are closely spaced jumps. Bikers ride in a series of heats, or preliminary races. They're in the air more than they are on the ground. The top finishers in each heat square off in the main race. Those that do not qualify are given two more chances to make the final event. The first rider over the finish line in Supercross wins.

When there's a crash don't expect riders to brake. Unlike in NASCAR racing, when a motocross rider flips or has an accident, the other riders continue on their way.

The Nic-Nac

In the 1990s, Jeremy McGrath, nicknamed "Showtime," performed some amazing tricks on his motorcycle. His most famous was called the Nic-Nac. McGrath took one foot off a footpeg and swung that leg around to the opposite side, all while flying high above the track.

Supermoto

Supermoto racers use off-road bikes on paved roads and dirt trails. The bikes have special tires that can grip both surfaces.

Hold on to your helmet. And hold on to your bike! Freestyle is a high-flying version of motocross, an anything-goes jumping competition. Freestyle, or FMX, didn't become a competitive event until the 1990s. Race promoters scheduled freestyle shows with cash prizes after seeing the crowd go wild when riders began running "jump-offs" during breaks in motocross events.

When the freestyle movie *Crusty Demons of Dirt* was released on DVD in 2001, the sport's popularity took off. The movie featured riders soaring over sand dunes, houses, buses, and much more. The sport boomed. Many motocross riders crossed over to freestyle events. The tricks became more daring and more complicated. The sport reached new heights when Caleb Wyatt succeeded in doing the first successful backflip in 2002.

Freestyle riders use most of the same gear as

Freestyle riders are always pushing the envelope developing the next best trick.

motocross racers, including helmets and pants. Most wear knee and elbow pads. A few will wear protective body armor if they are performing dangerous tricks. The bikes, however, are modified to weigh less to make them easier to maneuver.

FMX racers are awarded points for how good a rider looks when doing his or her tricks. Judges also award points based on the difficulty of the trick and how well one trick flows to the next.

Here are some of the more popular FMX tricks:

Double Grab

- **Can Can:** Rider takes one foot off the footpeg and raises a leg up and over the seat so that both legs are on the same side of the bike.
- **Cliff Hanger:** While soaring through the air, the rider stands straight up and catches the underside of the handlebars with his toes.
- **Double Grab:** Grab the rear of the bike with both hands while extending legs.
- **Superman:** The rider releases both feet and kicks them out.

- Surfer: The rider, holding on to the handlebar with both hands, stands up on the seat of the bike as a surfer stands on a surfboard.
- Tsunami: The rider performs a headstand in front of the handlebars.

Cliff Hanger

Off-road MX racers encounter many types of challenging terrains during races.

Off-road is a demanding form of MX. Racers have to be at the top of their game, physically and mentally. Off-road racing is an endurance sport, as racers battle the **terrain** and not necessarily each other. Off-roaders participate in a variety of events, including:

- Enduros: These races are run on wooded trails and dirt roads. Riders start the race one minute apart. They follow a set of instructions and try to maintain an average speed.

- Hare Scrambles and Cross-Country: Both races are held on long courses over rugged landscape. Riders complete a set of laps. Sometimes they are timed. The typical race lasts about two hours. Riders have to maintain a fast pace and have to be tough enough to withstand such a long race.

- Endurance or Desert: These races can last a day or more. Riders race from point-to-point. They receive points when checking in at each location. The quickest rider overall wins. Endurance riders must know when to pull in for a pit stop without losing valuable minutes. In some races, a team of riders will use one bike. The Dakar Rally, a multi-stage race, is one of the most difficult endurance races.

The soft desert sands make tight turns difficult at high speed.

GEAR UP

In motocross, the most important piece of gear is the bike. Nothing else comes close. Riders don't need a motorcycle with blazing speed; they need a bike that can bound over hills and slosh through mud without breaking down.

Tires have to be bigger than those used on street machines. They have wide tracks for better **traction**. Brakes can't give out. Shock absorbers on the back and front of the bike, along with the rest of the **suspension system**, have to be tough enough to withstand constant pounding. A good suspension system makes the bike easier to handle and brake.

Thick tire treads help churn through dirt and mud. The chain makes the tires spin.

Early Bikes

Like race cars, motocross bikes have evolved, or changed, over the years. The first scramble bikes in Europe weighed nearly 400 pounds (181 kilograms). The bikes were so heavy they often got stuck in the mud. Riders had to get off to push them out. Moreover, it wasn't a smooth ride. Shock absorbers were not added until the 1960s.

As the years passed, bike technology kept up with the demands of the sport. Through trial and error, engineers and riders eventually built the sleek racing machines of today.

This illustration shows how pistons move up and down in cylinders. This can happen thousands of times per minute.

If motocross is all about the bike, then the bike is all about the engine. Motocross bike engines are either two-strokes or four-strokes. For decades, the four-stroke engine was the main motorcycle powerhouse. The term comes from the number of moves the engine makes to create power. Each corresponds to one full stroke of the piston inside a **cylinder**.

The first stroke occurs when the piston moves down. It draws in a fresh mixture of fuel and air. The second stroke is when the piston moves up. It squeezes the fuel and air. During the third stroke, the **spark plug** fires. That ignites the fuel. The fuel expands.

It drives the piston downward. During the fourth stroke, the piston drives the engine exhaust out of the cylinder.

Four-strokes ruled until the two-strokes came along. Two-stroke engines combine all of the elements of a four-stroke engine in only two strokes of the piston. As a result, two-strokes produce more power than a four-stroke engine of the same capacity.

Here's a tight look at part of a motorcycle engine. The gears turn the heavy chain to spin the wheels.

The power of the four-stroke engine helps riders get the power for jumps.

The two-stroke engines took over the sport in the 1960s. The defining moment came in 1963 when Vlastimil Valek won the opening moto of the Czech 500 Grand Prix using a two-stroke. But the sport began shifting back to four-strokes in the 1980s when several state governments banned

American Gary Bailey was a star in the 1960s riding this 250cc bike.

the high-polluting two-strokes. Although the two-strokes were not barred from motocross competition, many bike makers started producing cleaner-burning four-strokes, which most riders now use in 250cc and 450cc classes.

HIGH-TECH GEAR

Much of today's riding gear is made from space-age materials designed to keep the rider safe and let them go fast. Racers wear helmets, gloves, and protection made from many high-tech substances. Some helmets, for example, are fashioned from **fiberglass** and carbon composites. Fiberglass is heat and fire resistant. The

Full helmets and goggles or face shields protect riders from flying debris.

glass fibers are woven tightly together. Composites are made when two or more materials combine to form a stronger substance.

Engineering the gear is also a science. Engineers design the shells of the helmets to absorb impacts. The energy generated by an impact is **diffused**, or spread out, before it reaches the driver's head. In addition, some helmets and motocross vests are made of Kevlar, a super-strong material woven together like a tight spider web. Some bulletproof vests are made of Kevlar. Body suits are made from comfortable and breathable mesh with protection areas for the chest, shoulders, elbows, and upper arms. Some suits feature a hard, plastic breastplate to protect the rider's chest.

The steel toes of these heavy-duty riding boots let drivers use their feet to push around tight turns.

The Zero X climbs up hills using electricity instead of gasoline.

SILENCE OF THE BIKES

What might the motocross bike of the future look like? Actually, the future is here. Some MX bikes are powered by electricity, not gasoline. Neal Saiki was one of the pioneers of electric-powered bikes. For years, Neal worked to build an electric bike that could compete with the two- and four-strokes. As a result, he developed the Zero X.

Saiki eliminated the engine and exhaust. There's no noise and no smoke. The bike runs on lithium batteries rather than gas. The 2012 Zero X weighed in at 215 pounds (97.5 kilograms) and had a top speed of 56 miles (90 kilometers) per hour.

Other companies also produce electric bikes. An Austrian company, KTM, a heavyweight in motocross, began selling the Freeride in Europe in 2014. One version of the bike, which is powered by a 300-volt battery, can reach speeds up to 50 miles (80 kilometers) per hour.

Electric MX

Electric bikes replacing gasoline-powered motorcycles in motocross competitions is unlikely. Perhaps they don't have to. In 2014, the second E-MX Race of Champions was held in Belgium. It is the top race for electric motocross bikes. Organizers hope to make it an annual event.

THE STARS

like many other sports, motocross has a rich history of outstanding athletes. Although European riders dominated the sport for years, they began facing Americans with immense talent. On July 4, 1969, Gary Bailey became the first American to defeat a group of European riders during the Firecracker Grand Prix at Saddleback Park in California.

Champion rider Gary Bailey was the first MX legend from the US.

If Gary was a racing legend, then Ricky Carmichael was a racing god. Ricky, who retired in 2007, turned pro in 1996 when he was 16. He finished the year in eighth place and was voted Rookie of the Year in the 125cc class. By the time of his retirement nine years later, Ricky held the record for the most combined wins of

Ricky Carmichael was a winner at every level of MX racing.

any rider in the history of motocross and Supercross. He was so good that he had two perfect AMA Motocross Championship seasons, winning every race.

Kerry Kleid Makes History

When Kerry Kleid was 21 in 1971, she became the first woman to be issued a professional motocross license by the AMA. She was also the first woman to be inducted into the AMA Hall of Fame.

Women's motocross has had its share of superstars, too. Sue Fish, nicknamed "The Fly Fish," was the first woman to compete against the men. Sue dominated female motocross during the 1970s and 1980s. She won two National Motocross Championships in 1976 and 1977.

Sue and others paved the way for a flood of female riders, including Tarah Geiger, who won the first women's Supercross at the 2008 X Games. She won two silver X Games medals in 2010 and 2011. She also finished fourth in 2013 at the X Games

Marissa Markelon is an up-and-coming champion.

Tarah Geiger puts her foot down for balance as she handles a tight turn.

Women's Enduro X Final in Barcelona, Spain.

Marissa Markelon is another champion, winning the 2014 AMA Women's Motocross Championship. She was two points behind defending champ Mackenzie Tricker and five points ahead of Kylie Fasnacht.

Ken Roczen zoomed out of Germany to become one of today's top MX racers.

TODAY'S STARS

It seems that each racing season brings a fresh crop of riders to the top of their sport. The most talked about rider in recent years has been Ken Roczen. In 2014, he won the Lucas Oil Pro Motocross Championship 450. He also won two 450 Supercross races, including the season opener.

Look for Jeremy Martin to move up to the 450cc class now that he has mastered the 250cc class.

Jeremy Martin is another motocross standout. He has taken home many amateur titles and awards. He made his pro debut in 2012. Although he was sidelined for the season with a shoulder injury, he came through in 2014 when dominated the first five motos of the 250 Class in the Lucas Oil Pro Motocross Championship. By the end of the season, he was the top rider in that class.

Ryan Dungey is one of the veterans of motocross. He won the AMA's Rookie of the Year Award in 2007 for Supercross/Motocross, working and training with Ricky Carmichael. He came in second to Ken Roczen in the 2014 Motocross Championship.

Ryan Dungey is successful in stadium Supercross and outdoor Motocross.

James "Bubba" Stewart, right, became the first African-American to win a major motocross championship. That happened in 2007 when he took home the AMA Supercross crown. He did so again in 2009. James, who still races, is a hard and aggressive rider, traits that he has passed on to his brother, Malcolm. Malcolm originally wanted to be a professional bass fisherman, but instead settled on motocross, making his professional debut in 2011.

Go for the Moto Gold

The Lucas Oil Pro Motocross Championship is the premier racing series in motocross. It is a 12-event series that begins in May and ends in August. The AMA Supercross Championship is a 17-race series that begins in January and ends in May, just before the Motocross Championship series begins.

GOING FOR THE WIN!

All the big names get a good jump at Angel Stadium. Andrew Short maneuvers into the early lead. Ken Roczen is behind. Still, the German isn't about to go quietly. What happens next underscores why he is one of the best. "Boy, this one is as tight as they come through that first corner," the announcer says. "They're still deciding it."

Ken Roczen wears a GoPro camera on his helmet to capture the ride.

Finally, Roczen makes his move. He creeps up on Davi Millsaps and passes him. "There's second place changing hands." Ken then takes aim at Andrew.

The whine of the cycles echoes. Suspension systems rattle. Tires churn up the dirt. Ken won here a couple of weeks ago, leading all 20 laps. This time he will have to work a bit harder.

Bursting from the pack, Ken finds some clear dirt to build up speed for a jump.

Ken Roczen soars above the competition to win at Anaheim.

Finally, he makes a decision. "Roczen thinking about the lead," the announcer yells. Ken and his Suzuki fly off a hill and pass Andrew. "He's got it," says the announcer's partner. Not long after, Andrew flies head first over the bars and crashes onto the track with a thud that no one can hear.

Ken Roczen proudly displays his trophy and rewards from a win.

As for Ken, he opens up a sizeable lead. Ryan Dungey moves into second and tries to chip away. He never does. Ken crosses the finish line with a jump that seems to go on forever. Ken and his Suzuki have started the new Supercross season at the top. Over the coming weeks, he'll see if they can stay there.

GLOSSARY

checkered flag (CHEK-erd FLAG): a black-and-white checked banner traditionally waved at the end of a motor sports race

cylinder (SILL-en-der): a tube-shaped sleeve that houses a piston in an engine where the fuel and air mixture is drawn in so it can be burned

diffused (dih-FUZED): spread out

exhibition (ex-ih-BISH-un): a performance of a sport that doesn't count toward regular standings

exploits (EX-ployts): daring action

fiberglass (FYE-ber-glass): fibers of glass that are woven together

maneuver (mah-NOO-ver): steer or form the direction of

spark plug (SPARK PLUG): the device that ignites the fuel/air mixture in the cylinder

suspension system (suss-PEN-shun SIS-tum): a system of shock absorbers and springs that connects a vehicle to its wheels and allows for a smooth ride

terrain (tuh-RANE): an area of land or ground

throttle (THROT-uhl): the mechanism used to control the flow of fuel into an engine

traction (TRAK-shun): the ability of a tire to grip a surface; or the ability of an idea to gain interest and popularity

variations (vare-ee-AY-shuns): degree of differences

INDEX

SHOW WHAT YOU KNOW

1. What year was the scramble born?

2. Which European rider thrilled American audiences in the 1960s?

3. What is the difference between a four-stroke and two-stroke engine?

4. What is an enduro?

5. What is freestyle MX?

WEBSITES TO VISIT

www.motorcyclemuseum.org

www.adventure.howstuffworks.com/outdoor-activities/snow-sports/heli-skiing.htm

www.promotocross.com/motocross/history

ABOUT THE AUTHOR

John Perritano is an award-winning journalist and author who has written dozens of nonfiction and fiction books for adults, kids, and teens, including many relating to sports. He lives in Southbury, Connecticut, on "Big Dog Farm" with a menagerie of pets, including albino frogs.

Meet The Author!
www.meetREMauthors.com

www.rourkeeducationalmedia.com

PHOTO CREDITS: Cover © TKTKTKT; Dreamstime.com: Rozum 6; Ttretjak 7; Southernstar71 12; Jlombard 13; Hamik 14; Graphiccancer 15; Natursports 16; Christian Bertrand 21; Cristian Saulean 22; EugeneSergeev 27; Appler 26; Paul Domanski 28; jurjcorr 30, 31; Erness 33; BStefanov 38, 43; Anthony Aneese Totah Jr. 40. MotorcycleMuseum.org: 8. Uppsala MCK: 11. Mortons Archive: 8, 9, 10; Courtesy Gary Bailey: 29, 34. Dollar Photo Club: Sergiogen 19; Will06photos 23; EugeneSergeev 24; José16 25, title page; Gontar 29. Courtesy Zero X Motorcycles: 32. PrimalXOnline: 36; Red Bull Content Pool: 37; Newscom: Diane Moore/SM 735 17, 35; Charles Mitchell/Icon Sportswire CFX 39, 44; J. Caseres/EFE 45. Shutterstock: Warren Price Photography 41.

Edited by: Keli Sipperley
Produced by Shoreline Publishing Group
Design by: Bill Madrid, Madrid Design

Library of Congress PCN Data

Motocross Racing / John Perritano
(Intense Sports)
ISBN 978-1-63430-442-9 (hard cover)
ISBN 978-1-63430-542-6 (soft cover)
ISBN 978-1-63430-630-0 (e-Book)
Library of Congress Control Number: 2015932637

Printed in the United States of America, North Mankato, Minnesota

Also Available as:
ROURKE'S
e-Books